A DIFFICULT
ANIMAL

A DIFFICULT ANIMAL

LISA LUTWYCHE

SADDLE ROAD PRESS

A Difficult Animal
© 2016 by Lisa Lutwyche

Saddle Road Press
Hilo, Hawai'i
www.saddleroadpress.com

Author photograph by Kristi Crutchfield Cox
Cover image by Lisa Lutwyche
Book design by Don Mitchell

ISBN 978-0-9969074-3-9
Library of Congress Control Number: 2016948361

In memory of my Father
William Stokking

(1933 — 2014)

Contents

IV Equinox Eve

V Sanctuary

I

TAKING THE MUSIC

Taking the Music

Fathers and daughters are a difficult animal,
full of love and confusion, with hidden teeth.
What I wanted most from him was love

for my mother. I knew he loved in me
what was like him, a wicked humor,
love of water and sky, fishing, and stories.

His hands held the power to move hearts.
Handsome, charismatic, exacting;
he mesmerized, drove people to their feet.

I watched him on bright stages from dark
wings. Bach Suite for Cello, sad threnody,
swept daily through my childhood.

My parents parted. Left nothing but a bitter
taste. For thirty years a stepmother my own age
filled a place in him I only partly understood.

I folded her in, made her family
of my heart. She raised their sons, my brothers.
When she left him, he telephoned my mother.

A rediscovery too late. One dazzling recital,
one last audience applauding — and my mother
found him on his kitchen floor. I have, now,

what I wanted. He loves my mother.
He holds her hand, smiles, shrugs amiably as
she feeds him. She feeds him; tenderness,

a thing I'd longed for. He tilts in his wheelchair.
Bewhiskered, wrinkled tee shirt stained,
unable to speak. He lifts his sea-green

eyes to mine. Saying — what? Mostly his eyes
are empty. I close mine, strain to remember
the rich swell of sound as he took up his bow,

cocked his ear to the body; a hollowness
of glued wood and strings — listen...
But the arm twists, taking the music away.

THAT DAMN SWAN

I hid from mirrors. I could always
take off my glasses, hide in the blur —
excuse my clumsiness. Drown in books.
"You're just an Ugly Duckling,"

my mother said. The moral being: Swan.
Meant as comfort, to soothe a needy child,
it fixed me on a future self. Promise of beauty.
Three daughters. Comparisons inevitable.

Neither "Smart" nor "Pretty," I wore my mantle
of "Eldest" like an itchy cloak. Looked
after my sisters as our parents' marriage died.
An inelegant ballet. Their own Dying Swan.

The family spread across the continent.
I left the Duckling and her sisters far behind.
I pretend I don't remember. I dodge photos,
avoid my reflection, cultivate my intellect.

But here she is again, in a dark room
behind the mirror. She waits, watching the sky
and the door, begging me, anyone, to turn her
into that damned, someday-promised Swan.

MUSICAL RAPTURE

My mother's piano in the sleeping house,
lovely and tortured. Passages
played over and over until they obey.
And when the music does her will,
the hair raises on my stick skinny arms.
My ugly cheeks rain with tears.

Rapture wraps me, wide-awake,
all colors and rocking waves of aching.
I'll break the spell if I go to her,
playing downstairs, alone.
But I want to tell her someone
is listening to her wasted music.

Even now it comes to me. Chopin. Bartok.
My sister's breathing, my mother's hands.
This feeling so like pain —
dangerous, evocative, recalling
a past I've never understood.
She played only when my father wasn't there.

But I remember also when they played together —
cello, piano, my held breath.

The Cellist

He wraps his arms around her.

Even in front of my mother.
Later, in front of my step-mother,
my sisters, half-brothers, me.

She is all curves and glowing,
deep mahogany and warm ebony,
a voice that weeps, laughs, sighs

only for him.
His scandalous affection as shameless
as her flagrant devotion.

Every day, sometimes several times,
they don't care who sees them,
he caresses her with cloth and hands.

In front of hundreds of strangers,
he takes her in his loving embrace,
places his fingers on her neck,

draws his bow across her body
and she sings.
Oh God, how she sings.

ALLEGRO APPASSIONATO

What child knows she's lucky? Watching my parents on
stage, I felt bereft, even jealous, not proud. Now I have
only the recordings.

Alive again, playing on a small screen,
my father pours *Allegro Appassionato*
into a room of strangers. More honey than notes.

Those people couldn't know the treasure
they received. He made it look so easy. Each
of his wives — elegant, attentive at their pianos,

accompanied the same *Saint-Saëns* over
years while he blazed, black-clad, inscrutable,
behind the shining russet of his cello.

My magical father. The night he died,
my fingers tapped my pillow, making notes
sound in my exhausted head — my internal piano,

intervals learned from a childhood spent
in lessons — when playing was working. In my house, the
next morning, I went downstairs

to my real piano, dusty, beautiful, neglected thing.
My hands rendered a piece of Bach they'd never played
before. Music — but the rest of that day

was the silence he'd left for us. "Think of things
that made you laugh," a friend said. The smile
at the edges of his voice, the crinkled corners

of his eyes that always gave the game away.
He was *Allegro*: "brisk and uplifting."
He could make an entire orchestra laugh.

Then his face grew serious. A beat of silence
as he bent his bow to the waiting strings —
and that moment when the audience was his.

GREAT-GRANDMOTHER ANNETTA

Once I learned to watch her hands
I forgot to be afraid of her whiskers.
Twisted driftwood fingers

tied with the blue ropes of her veins.
Skin like draped patterned silk,
or spotted wax, melted, crinkled,

folded over sinewy bands.
Quick machines, those deft fingers
snapped green beans like cold jade,

"pop-clink, pop-clink, pop-clink"
into a thick white bowl with chipped edges.
Smiling, she murmured responses

to my breathless little-girl questions.
"What was it like back then?"
Her hands stilled, crossed on her apron.

She sighed, eyes closed, remembering.

GENTLE WATCH

"...and they might now breathe above..." ~ Annie Finch

The dead grandmothers watch me.

Perhaps they breathe above,
wander with me through mistakes,
shaking their celestial heads sometimes.
The grandmothers didn't mingle in life.

But now, where they breathe,
where they hover above and around me,
they laugh behind their hands
or weep at my outrages.

Their presence is a soft constant,
informing my gestures. The way I cook,
the way I take my tea,
the dip and loop of my crochet hook.

No answers for my questions,
just the things their own grandmothers
imparted to their fingers — that, watching them,
my hands echo, my daughter's hands, my son's.

The way we chop an onion, hold a warm cup.
Sometimes I look out a window,
over a kitchen sink, dreaming,
and there, out of the corner of my eye, a smile.

Requiem for a Nuisance

An autumn night: cool, misty tang,
road wet and treacherous, hazard lights
ahead. I stopped. Inside, lit by the dashboard,
a woman crying.

"It's still alive. I think it's a baby."
She pulled off the road, joined me
in the dazzle. "There. Do you see?
The mother is watching us."

A doe, two fawns, waiting, ghostly, in the trees.
At my feet, wild eyed, bewildered,
a yearling thrashed. His tender tongue
grazed lacerating asphalt.

Buds of antlers buried in his velvet brow,
I felt his coarse fur, readying for winter,
ran my fingers along his neck, his trembling flank,
felt his racing heart, stroked his silken ears.

Only a cut on his pink lip
as if his mother had recently washed it.
Did she love him, despite her needy younger ones?
I looked at her, as she watched me.

He gasped, a long, grinding moan, and quieted.
His heartbeat slowed. Stopped.
Wordlessly, we dragged his shattered body
from the road, pillowed his head.

His eyes wouldn't close
so we covered his face with soft, dried grass.
When I saw him the next day, he seemed asleep,
lying in the gentle bed of leaves we'd made.

People say they're a nuisance on the roadways.
I only know the way he felt to touch
and how his mother's eyes looked into mine
from the shadows.

II

INVISIBLE

HONEYSUCKLE MIST

Home from air-conditioned office mayhem,
the family waits in our sweltering house for dinner.
My clothes hang hot, like an extra skin.
Even out of them, my own skin feels too thick.

I don't want to hear my insistent dog, but I do,
so I take on even hotter boots to wade
into the early summer muck of a creekside yard.
The dog yanks, gnats dangle in my eyelashes,

I watch the muddy stumping
of my grass fringed boots, dragging —
until a tender drop of rain touches my neck,
a neon slice of lightning raises my eyes

and I see the wet, amber tangle of woodpath,
the filigree of ferns embracing in the rising steam,
leaves dancing, bobbing, twirling in the droplets,
and the black-webbed purple structure of the trees.

Birds drown distant thunder with their worship,
filling the green veils. If I could live in this
honeysuckle mist, in this singing, cool dominion —
but the dog shakes himself, hops

pulls and whimpers. Spell shattered,
we go inside, where, in the torpid air,
everything is suspended
waiting for my tired, enacting hands.

MATH TEARS

I ride into my childhood
on the track of a tear
inside my son's glasses.

The smell of steam
and dish detergent.
Taste of defeat.

I am eight or nine. Under
cold sweaty fingers
my math papers crackle.

My mother's soapy hands
jab at my homework.
I feel her anguish.

The wet paper curls,
clings to the flawless shine
of a plastic laminate table.

My feet tap and scrape linoleum.
Tears of frustration cloud
my pink cats-eye glasses.

My sister plinks the Steinway.
Finches chitter in their pretty cage
to Vietnam on black and white TV.

Now — my son's face pleads,
"It's fifty, right?
Isn't it fifty, Mommy?"

MTV blares colors and noise from
the living room. And I understand
my mother's helpless, soapy jabs.

SWEETBITTER UNMANAGEABLE CREATURE
WHO STEALS IN
~Sappho (fragment 130)

Two weeks early, she will be difficult.
She is cut from me. Savage arrival.
I would do anything for this child I don't yet know.

Nothing will be easy for the sweetbitter child.
Our house is a drafty, ruined, unfinished place,
demolished in my sour parting from her father.

Disillusioned by all the wreckage, I make
a home so craving of order that the unruly creature
rebels, resists, and steals herself away.

Now, following Sappho's sweetbitter path,
she inhabits a country intolerant of who she loves.
But my daughter lifts her determined chin.

Little poet, artist, beautiful muse, firstborn child. My
sweetbitter unmanageable creature
will dissolve the bitter with her sweet soul.

INVISIBLE

so if I am
        invisible
let me twirl
        around your faces
laughing
        teasing
let me dance naked
and shout
forbidden dreams

if I am
invisible
(hell) let me steal
Diamonds and Vermeers

let me hijack
a Porsche
(mysterious
behind darkened
windows)

if I am invisible
let me speak
aloud my shy
and unprotected
love

that hangs
unanswered
that I offered
all my life

LATE AGAIN

The oldest child is four.
Cozy in pink winter fleece she goes outside.
Daddy paces by the car.

He buckles her seat belt in choppy silence.
When he asks, "Where's your mother?"
she knows not to answer him.
She watches Daddy walk into the house.

She knows Mommy is kneeling
by her Baby Brother. She knows
Mommy fussed him into his snowsuit,
cuddled him, cajoled him.

Mommy kissed her forehead,
squeezed her mittened hand,
sent her outside. She felt
Mommy's fear and sadness.

Now she hears Daddy's shouts
and Mommy's crying.
She jumps in her car-seat
when the kitchen door slams.

Glass shatters. A scary sound,
like something on TV.
Daddy gets behind the wheel.
He stares at his own tapping fingers.

Mommy comes out of the house.
She leans in and meets the child's eyes.
A promise of quiet passes between them.
Baby Brother is all huge eyes.

When Mommy sits in front
the child sees splinters of glass
sparkling in Mommy's hair.
It could be pretty but she knows it isn't.

Mommy stares out her window,
fingers to lips. The tires pop gravel.
The car jumps. The child holds on.

"Late again," Daddy says.

CARTOON RAGE

Sunday morning
TV with my littlest

calm, silly
drinking coffee
daughter sleeping late

along comes
their dad and somehow
it starts

rubber knees
funny bones wobbly
from my anger

hands floating
not fists
(they don't know how)

helpless unformed words
hover and circle

like birdies
and stars
in a cartoon
after
the sledge hammer

CHOPPING ONIONS

the issue was not the issue.

the issue was that she
        wouldn't say it,
        wouldn't hear it,
would not be made
        to receive it;
and so his words
        punished, slashed,
        tore and gored

and she was silent.

she wanted the children
        not to hear it;
she wanted the children
        not to be mystified
        by seeing her outrage
or her tears.

so she found a way
        an explanation
in this cool evisceration;
bloodless
        destruction

in onion tears

CAREWORN

Deaths of dreams
are tilled across my forehead,
grooves that deepen
while I watch

I wear the days, the years,
in layers on my face
sagging at the edges
of my chin

Late mortgage payments,
nights before deadlines,
lost love, and loves
I dreamed

gather on my back
to strain
and hunch
my narrow shoulders

All the times
he came home angry,
all the times my children
weren't ready

in the morning,
all the times I fell asleep
harried and hollow
have tugged me

into a soft satin looseness
I am an outdated dress
worn by the woman
I might have been

SUMMER DREAMS, SPIDER PROMISES

The air hangs thick with my own promises,
cloying, unrelenting, woven long ago.

I wove them with the hopeful patience
of a spider. I cast them into the humid air

to cling, uncompromising,
and the strands will not release me.

Something about this hot, unforgiving
summer makes me think of old dreams,

old summers. Nauseated by swallowed sobs
I watch the sun plummet, earlier and earlier.

Lightning tickles the edges of sky
like dreams that will shatter with thunder.

The air dangles with unspoken promise,
glimmering like the soft blue edge of dusk.

In the early throes of this dying summer,
the sparkle of fireflies almost gone,

I watch a spider struggle in the last
frail strings of her rain torn web.

The Wife

and so his words
>> struck her face
>> though not yet
his hands

and so his coldness
>> fell into her hair
>> like flakes
of snow

and so his indifference
>> surrounded her
>> like petals
dead flowers

and so her smiles
>> were no longer
>> returned.
and so frowns haunted

her lips which once
>> craved his kisses
>> and tears froze
in her eyes

and so icy with hurt
>> she knew
>> this was how
it would be

and so she was his wife.

III

CONTROLLED DESCENT

BODY OF NO

No. It is not a word. It is my whole body.
No. I am closed to him.
I am not his to take.

I cinch the drawstring on my sweatpants
with a square knot. Tight
around my jutting hips.

No. My body is no. My body is denial.
This is the only place in this house
I am meant to sleep.

My children are upstairs.
I say the word. "No."
I say, "Please."

The sweatpants are yanked away.
My breasts are squeezed.
My ear is panted into and I

am up on all fours how he likes it.
Safe from his face, from
the impersonal brutality of his lips.

Night after night.
Year after year. And I keep the peace.
For the sake of my children,

our children, asleep upstairs.
I am his for his demands.
I am meat.

I am up on all fours,
taken from behind
and he is done and the

No
is whispered into the mattress
with my tears.

PROVOCATION

"You want me to hit you."

Was I intended to admire his restraint
in the face of my stupidity,
clumsiness, sloppiness, stammering,

and questionable attitude?
My constant provocation
of the fury that was his habit?

I was told what was good for me.

All I had to do was to
listen, anticipate, behave,
drop everything — NOW.

"You want me to hit you."

I took my beatings on the inside.
There were no bruises to ice,
nothing to stitch, nothing to show.

There was no one to help.

Threats. Smashed window. Torn sleeve.
Something thrown, something broken.
Demonstrations of what might happen.

"You want me to hit you."
Would any help have come if he had?

SLANT

Here in the slanted light of winter day
the wind's teeth cruelly chew my face and ears.
My fingers curl to keep the cold away;
my eyes sting with unaffected tears.
It's snowing now before the solstice date.
I wrap myself in work, I read and write,
observe my inward mood and, watchful, wait
for early dark to bring my secret night.
The silhouetted trees melt into gloom.
The moon begins its certain, upward, slide.
A cheerful fire softly warms the room
as gentle cats push close on either side.
I must get strong before the freezing starts.
I glove my hands. I shield my shivering heart.

THE YELLOW ROOM

My daughter isn't yet eighteen,
so we're taken to the yellow room.
Teddy bears and clowns
cavort across the walls.

Her outfit, thrift shop clothes she loves,
is motley and too-big. I wear black.
We wait, stiff and wordless.

The doctor inspects her forearms,
peers up at my sweet girl's face, and frowns.
"Tell me about this."
"I did these with a candle.
Those are cuts. This one, the cross,
I did with incense."

I look away. A mobile swims
in lazy circles over the infant scale.
I can almost feel my little girl again,
warm weight in my lap.

Oh, could I burn my own flesh?

Advice, a referral for help,
and the doctor leaves. I catch
my daughter's worried look.
I snort, "God, I hate clowns!"
She rolls down her sleeves.

Our smiles fade.

Controlled Descent

if you want to know your monsters, dive deep

For a controlled descent you must invite the water,
chamber by slow chamber. You must fill for ballast

but control it. Once I went too fast.
Several of my crew were drowned.

I was swept backwards by the water's force,
hatch door overwhelmed, helpless.

I can still feel the slippery wrist of the last man.

We continued, knowing it was the only way
the depths could be explored

Bring weapons, should you venture out. Breathe
slowly and hover between the pressure of descent

and the craving you will surely feel for light

Remember this or your vessel will implode. One
danger if you stay too long below, the portholes
might occlude,

you could lose your taste for sun

Let your periscope dare the surface first. Sweep
the long horizon. Be sure to leave your discoveries
undisturbed beneath the waves.

promise to forget them

The Watch

I have the watch tonight.
Out in the rage of lightning
under the punishing
turmoil of the sky,

I ache to close my eyes
just to shut
the purple lids
heavy as hatch covers,

to curl, warm
beneath the decks
where gentle lamplight flickers
where pillows beckon

where I could rock
and sleep. The cold wind,
the slicing wicked rain,
all the forces

against which
I guard in this watch,
that leave me
naked, shivering,

I could just close
the purple doors
and sleep, warm forever
to watch no more.

Blue Moon

Now the blue moon wanes,
melting into her second
half, sapphire fading

to white clarity.
If her rareness is a thing
to wish upon, then

my hope takes wing.
I watch her rise. I fling my
dreams at her, and wait.

IV

EQUINOX EVE

RECIPE

(or How Divorce is Like Making Chicken Soup)

Divide it first
While cold
Clean water
      Boils

Salt well
Season to
      Distaste

Add parts
Back in: giblets,
Neck
      All of them.

Savor the scent.
Simmer for twenty
      Months

When meat falls
From bones
      Discard them

Examine
Tediously
      For veins
      Sinew.

Find the heart
      Eat it.

Brewing the Witch

It is so easy now to let
the dark vapors swallow her.
She stirs, slowly, her sour,

unaccustomed bitterness,
savors the poisonous taste
that pinches her features

into this wicked mask,
deepens the lines etched by the acid
of her years of powerlessness.

Her lips peel into a grimace
that refuses to weep,
her dark hair tangled

by her own despairing fingers.
She picks up the requisite hunch
from the hopelessness

that racked her shoulders
for decades. The black cape is woven
of her rage. It wraps her,

swirling around her cauldron.
She stirs in the deep secret
of her untapped strength.

Careful of mirrors,
she brews the witch
she needs to be.

ORION'S TEARS

Tears of Orion fall as crystals from the winter sky.
Snow coats the spindled grass.
The hush echoes with an owl's lament.

The owl's cry was the one thing my son
missed, later. He left the house, grabbing boxes
of what was his and his sister's.

He stepped carefully between his father and me,
between our trucks going opposite directions.
I watched the boy avoid our eyes.

Tears of Orion crash, spitting ice
in the moonless night. Orion kept me silent company so
many years — my only champion,

poised in the heavens, full of fury,
arrows pointed at all the waste, at all
my anguished nights. Tears of Orion fall

as wind-lashed rain. But now I reach
for my earthbound, mortal love
who holds me in his sleep as we dream of spring.

EQUINOX EVE

Dinner waits for my pen to stop.
Even in this quiet moment
I know something is about to happen.

The held breath of frozen ground
inhales sweet rain. Hungry roots stretch,
unsheathing stalks and blades.

Crocus lollipops celebrate,
already drifting
across the soggy straw of winter lawn.

The fire jitters happily.
Cats push close for extra warmth.
The light wanes to lavender outside.

Leafless tangles are cobwebbed with mist.
Pale paper banners of last year's beech
brighten the stiff grey anarchy of the woods.

As warm rain bathes the tired earth
and tickles dormant buds,
the rusty forest floor yields to the reckless green

of skunk cabbage and bluebells.
Tomorrow will be as long as tonight.
Tomorrow it will all be different.

Luna Moth

Lovely Luna, pinned eternally to fate
Pale green wings beating windows in their hush
I think of her, flesh healing as I wait.

What flower in darkness would have been her bait?
For me, my cancer chased the senseless rush.
Lovely Luna pinned eternally to fate.

Night after night death watched me long and late.
Would it be a scalpel's sweep or gentle brush?
As my flesh heals, I think of her and wait.

Searched and repaired, my stitched skin now relates
Symbols, like her wings, patterns red and lush.
Lovely Luna, pinned eternally to fate.

Arms out, wrists strapped, on the table I create
An image of the gentle insect crushed.
Lovely Luna, pinned eternally to fate
As my flesh heals and seals again I wait.

Blood Shadow

You think I don't know you're there,
but you're wrong.

I feel you always, the hot breath of your desire,
the cold creep of your fingers at my elbow.

They took one breast away, piece by agonizing piece. And,
since then, I detect your curious teeth at the other.

Perhaps, even now, you're growing in my blood,
my brain, my womb. Despite those pills I took,

by the reluctant, trembling handful.
I could pull the covers over my head, dodge down
alleyways, fly over oceans, put years between us.

But you will haunt my sleepless nights.
You'll trail me. I know.

You've had my name in your book for a long,
long time.

Awareness

As if October didn't already bring it all back.
The chill, the falling, tasting death on my tongue
along with woodsmoke.

Pink doesn't go with all the browns, reds
and yellows, but they mean well.
Their annual alert will save someone, somewhere.

I watched the trees that autumn.
Their brilliant colors were a bright rapture,
settling around their feet like a celebration.

If only I could have shed my breast
the way a tree slips her leaves.
A sigh, a tremor, and then she rests.

She sleeps through cold, harsh nights, knowing
she will wake with the flowers. No knife for her,
no pain, no terror. The letting go so easy.

FAMILY TREE

(of Berta and the two called Thyra)

Early in the last century, in an elegant city
of red bricks and peaceful courtyards,
my great-grandmother in Sweden
grew a furtive root in her child-weary body.

When it was discovered, my grandmother,
only daughter in a tribe of boys,
was here in this foreign place
with her new husband.

The immigrant girl anguished helplessly,
knowing her mother was bereft
of the gentle comfort of female hands,
knowing her mother's need, bravely denied.

Finally cured by the clumsy kiss of radium,
my great-grandmother lived long,
long enough to forgive her daughter's absence.
But not long enough to know

of the seeds left in her fruit.
Half a century later, her granddaughter,
found it again. It branched in her, from breast
to bone in stealthy, woody vines.

At my aunt's memorial I was healing
from the chopping of my own body's secret
tendrils. I carried the seeds into a new century.
But I buried them in salt and stone to die;

an offering of forgiveness
to the lonely woman in that red-bricked city
who yearned for an absent daughter,
long ago in our northern past.

Unbidden Stones

Listen, girl, you and I both know how it got there.

Remember when you used to get that big, tight knot of fear in your chest? How strong it was? Remember that hunted, haunted panic?

You were his quarry. Trapped in those scolding, hypnotic eyes. That feeling was so strong.

But you didn't scream it out. All that terror had to go somewhere. If it went nowhere, it stayed inside. Right where you said you felt it.

It's still in there, hardening.

He humiliated you in public, in front of his friends, your friends, his family, yours. In private, he diminished you. He took you down to nothing.

He stripped you of all power in front of the children. Is it any wonder they didn't always listen to you? They learned to manipulate you.

There! Where did you feel that?

Waves of shame that caught in your throat and tore at your insides. Sometimes, girl, didn't you just get so angry? You must have.

You learned that if you tossed a plastic tub of butter, he would throw a crockery bowl, or a chair, or even a table.

He would snort that righteous snicker at how
you lost control. He would leave you, all alone,
to clean it up.

And you'd be trembling. Back in your place.

But that rage was still in there, wasn't it? Seething.
Your solar plexus was hot with it. Energy that
stayed inside you and turned to micro crystals,

which gathered into tiny pebbles,

that grew to gravel and hung there, heavy,
in your breasts. Until they saw it. The doctor
showed it to you. Surreal, sitting on her desk,

grease pencil marks on your blue breasts.

Galaxies of tiny rocks, showing white, floating
in the utter dark universe of you. She told you
the degrees of possibility,

showed you the jagged clumps in right breast
and in left. She told you what your options were.
And you said, "cut them all out."

You picture yourself as a quarry of a different kind
now. You are a place that holds unbidden stones.

They will scatter if you don't stop them.

You will be a strip mine. You let the doctors do
with you what they will. You will be rid of the
rubble that man left inside of you.

Lighter, so much lighter.

Now, girl, you've started over.
This man, the man who loves you, will be holding
your hand. He will not care that your breasts are
dented, scarred, even excavated.

It seems to you that he may love
even the craters they leave behind.

V

Sanctuary

Pennsylvania Rain

I followed those taillights at 65 miles per hour,
pasted myself to the bumper of your rental car.
You called it "a dirty English night" and you
should know. I thought about you flying as

we raced to the airport.

You've had sky beneath your feet since the day
you jumped; the day you knew you loved me. Screaming
down the highway in the impossible rain, I remembered: I
did not meet you;

I recognized you.

What I knew of you from the first day was that
your eyes searched mine, probed me, and retreated; shy
British boy inside a man, with loneliness
that fit you with a gentle patina of daily use.

I knew your eyes were very blue.

I shut off my careful study at the mention
of a wife. But my heart remained alert, an unassigned
sentinel. The years passed, you
reached to me, polite, reticent, deferential.

We avoided each other's eyes — most of the time.

I watched you watch my life; a friend, a listener, little
gentle gestures when I suffered. My bitter life wore on
me; your life more empty by the year.
We never spoke of it

until the day I said I'd never have you, despite
the way my heart swelled, unbidden, inside me.
That day you leaped out of your plans, out of
your life, into my chaos and all my pain,

willing to leave your country for mine someday.

I followed the taillights of your rental car, just so we
could say goodbye. But the plane took off without you.
We yielded to our separate sleeps

while the wicked English wind lashed the Pennsylvania
rain.

DISTANCE

Open my eyes and wake again today,
To face whatever comes, force myself to stand.
Mirror mocks, not allowed to look away.
I'm off, unsteady, pulled by silken strands
of hope. Most days, I wake alone, but for
My nestled cat. The strength I need is missed.
I wash and dress, dragging through the door.
Some magic dawns, I find you and am kissed,
Sweet sunrise, and you, sending me aloft.
I fly those days, escaping every clutch.
Nothing stops me, knowing you wait, soft
Embrace for coming home. To sleep, your touch
Heals us both as we come to rest again.
Open my eyes tomorrow, long for when...?

THE WAIT

In tenderness
his long gentle
hands
awaken.

And, here,
she is
all
welcome.

Legs, hands, lips
she is alive
with wanting.
And he,

wanted,
takes her,
folds her
into

his trembling
limbs.
"How long,"
their bodies ask,

"How long
did we wait?"
And answer,
"Long enough."

Sanctuary

soft sun on my neck
as I pinch tiny weeds
from dark garden soil

behind the tiny white parsonage
we found to rent
warm, gentle winds

snatch at my hair
wooden clothespin
in my mouth

bed sheets snap
a breeze drifts across
tilled and untilled acres

soon the corn will be
tall enough to whisper
my tall daughter

suddenly hugs me
grinning as we pass
in a doorway

"mommy, you're so happy"
my son proclaims
as he pulls

spent petunias
confident there will be
more flowers

NEW

sweet soft air balms
my winter crackled hands

I drink it greedily
tasting the residue of sun

the evening falls
decorated with robin songs

and the glee of the first
tree frogs

I am as new as the slim
bone china moon

that rests gently alone
on the blue cloth of dusk

SECOND MARRIAGE

new habits in middle age
slipping into sleep with tangled limbs
folding together each night
still in a kind of wonder

he is all long, raw bones
thinning hair, beard mostly white
she, long-boned, too, with edges gone soft

dark blonde hair, ambushed wiry grey
their eyes match, almost
blue and bewitched, unbelieving

sometimes she sits him in a kitchen chair
for a haircut, dodging his playful grabs
while they talk poetry and politics

sometimes he tends her in the shower
combing out the snarls
of her heart and her history

Woman with a Birdcage

(of Kate, my grandmother, who was called *Geiske* before the crossing)

A birdcage, draped with a paisley shawl,
rests on a leather case. With it is a slim
sturdy young woman in brown wool.
Kate is called "handsome" but never beautiful.

To look at her, no one would guess how
frightened she is. She sits on a steamer trunk
as she waits, stoic in the cold, one gloved hand
on the cage.

It might be the same trunk her mother used
decades ago, coming to America from Holland.
Is she the same age her mother was?
Had her mother been this scared?

Her mother, Annetta, had never spoken of it.
Kate follows her husband halfway
across a continent, for a better life,
the same reason her parents crossed an ocean.

It's snowing. She remembers snow
on the countryside by frozen canals, horses
pulling sleighs on impossible ice, daring boys
on skates, clinging, squealing with joy.

She was called Geiske then, so young before
the crossing, before the farm and all the work.
The journey was harder on the rest of them
than it had been for her. So many of the old ones

leaned over the side, loved-ones clutching
so they wouldn't fall. Or they moaned below
in the vertical framework of their barracks.
She has never forgotten the terrible smells.

Geiske dashed across the decks with the other children;
two sisters from Poland, with pretty head scarves; Italian
twins chattering madly with each other; the Irish boy
with his red explosions of curls.

The babble of languages didn't matter.
The ship's crew gave them hard candies,
scraps of wood for boys' swords,
and dolls made from bits of rope.

In long skirts and heavy shoes, the women
nursed babies or rocked them absently.
The men smoked together in little groups,
without words, staring at the horizon, wondering.

Kate remembers excitement and cold sea air.
Today the cold is different, ice inside and out. The snow
has dwindled since New Jersey, picks up in Pennsylvania,
and all through the mountains it falls.

Even if she were not alone, she would not say
how ill she feels. Not like it was in the early months
but from the fear, closeness and rocking of the train.
The cage is so still now she is afraid to look inside.

Annetta had come with her to the station,
quiet tears in her eyes, cool, strong hands
pressing Kate's. "Go, be safe. He waits for you."
Kate smiles as the baby kicks inside her, restless

for his mother who will not complain of her own
restlessness. She eats only for the child. The lifeless cage
sickens her, too. She dares a glimpse. The yellow bird is
limp, a dulled grey, eyes closed,

it clings to its perch.
Just after dawn, St. Louis is deep with snow,
smoke and steam, vertical black and brown.
A big black automobile comes for her.

Finally, her husband's arms, all warmth and welcome as
he settles a wool blanket around her legs. She feels ugly,
bigger than she was when he'd seen her last,
filthy from the train.

To his eyes she is a treasure, beautiful
in her ripeness, in her trembling smile. He bustles
about her, takes her coat, her shoes. He brings her tea,
with milk, the way she always likes it when

she's feeling indisposed. She takes the cover from the
cage, places it in a slim shaft of sunlight and waits. The
bird huddles in a corner. She whistles softly and it stirs
and peers at her.

The bird's eyes blink, accusing, and close again.
Heartsick, she falls on the carefully made bed. The dense,
grey sky lifts away and she begins to warm. Fire newly lit,
husband content with his newspaper,

she sleeps completely. She dreams of sun on fields of
snow, in soft drifts, glittering like milled diamonds. She
feels again the movements of a ship
and the train, still tugging at her limbs.

She awakens to the sound of birdsong.

Resolution

A misty, ashen January day
turns to a dusk of lush wine purple, frigid,
streaked with the quiet dignity
      of winter trees.

Home from work, I'm soothed by warmth.
Here, in the tall brick surround,
feathery heads of flame poke between logs
      like nervous birds.

Soft crush of my cat,
breathing her rumbled joy,
puts my legs to sleep
      but how could I move her?

I've been reading poetry again.
Not folding laundry, cooking,
not planning, paying bills,
      or putting dishes away.

Not exercising. Instead
I've been watching words and the fire,
my husband near and quiet,
      letting the veil of night

fall, without even feeling guilty
about what I should be doing.
And I will
      I will do this again.

Acknowledgements

These poems have appeared, sometimes in slightly different forms, or were recognized by, the following publications or venues:

"sweetbitter unmanageable creature who steals in" was nominated for a Pushcart Prize in 2015.

"Brewing the Witch" and "sweetbitter unmanageable creature who steals in" were published in the anthology, *In the Questions: Poetry by and About Strong Women* (Spider Road Press, LLC) in 2015.

"Requiem for a Nuisance" was a finalist in the 2014 Atlanta Review International Poetry Competition, as well as a finalist in the 2013 *mslexia* Poetry Competition in the UK.

"Awareness" was published in *the cancer poetry project 2* (Tasora Books) in 2013.

"Orion's Tears" was published in *Minerva Rising* in 2012.

"Late Again" was published in *Unbreakable, and other Poems on Domestic Abuse*; a chapbook, the proceeds of which were donated to DAP (Domestic Abuse Project of Delaware County, PA), 2010.

"Unbidden Stones" won "Best Poem of the New Year" in 2009, in a 2nd Saturday Poets annual reading event in Wilmington, DE.

"Family Tree", "The Watch', "Invisible", "Careworn", "Summer Dreams", "New", "Recipe" were all published in *Mad Poets Review* between 1994 and 2009, in various forms (some under my former married name).

"Cartoon Rage" was published in *Hush, An Anthology of Poetry on Domestic Abuse*; a chapbook, the proceeds of which were donated to DAP (Domestic Abuse Project of Delaware County, PA), 2005.

"Math Tears" was a finalist in a poetry competition for *Runes* in 2003.

"The Watch" was nominated for a Pushcart Prize in 2000.

"Chopping Onions" was a Judge's Choice in a *Mad Poets Review* competition.

I also wish to thank: my husband, fellow poet Nicholas Lutwyche, for being my trusted and ever-patient first reader; "Written Remains" poetry critique group, spearheaded by Shannon Connor Winward; my beloved sister writers, Cathleen Delia Mulrooney and Jessa Marie Mendez-Velez; and A Room of Her Own Foundation (AROHO) for the incomparable Ruth Thompson.

ABOUT LISA LUTWYCHE

She received her MFA in creative writing from Goddard College in 2013. Poet, artist, produced playwright, writer, and actor, she has been anthologized and published across the US and in the UK since the1990s, including: *Mad Poets Review, Minerva Rising, Tamafyr Review, Falklands War Poetry, Sparrow's Trill, In the Questions — Poetry by and about Strong Women, cancer poetry project 2,* and *Fiction Vortex.*

Lisa was nominated for a Pushcart Prize for her poetry in 2000 and again in 2015. Her background includes a BFA in painting and a BA in

Kristi Crutchfield Cox

art history; twenty-two years in corporate architectural design; teaching art to special needs adults; working as an optician while in graduate school.

She is currently an adjunct Assistant Professor of English at Cecil College in Maryland and at Delaware County Community College in Pennsylvania.

CPSIA information can be obtained
at www.ICGtesting.com
Printed in the USA
BVHW032313310319
544193BV00001B/42/P